Lunch Boxes

Text copyright © 1988, 1999 Althea Braithwaite
Illustrations copyright © 1999 Christopher O'Neill

The moral rights of the author and of the illustrator
have been asserted.

This edition first published 1999 by Happy Cat Books,
Bradfield, Essex CO11 2UT

A CIP catalogue record for this book is available from
the British Library

ISBN 1 899248 48 X Paperback
ISBN 1 899248 43 9 Hardback

Printed in Hong Kong by Wing King Tong Co. Ltd

Lunch Boxes

Althea

Illustrated by Christopher O'Neill

Happy Cat Books

These children are all enjoying a school lunch. The food in this picture will help to keep us healthy.

MILK

COTTAGE CHEESE

COTTAGE CHEESE

Muesli Bar

Some children choose to bring a packed lunch.
What have they brought today?

Food gives us energy and keeps us warm.
It also makes us grow and keeps us healthy.

Most foods that we like contain a mixture of the
things that do us good.

Steven has tuna fish sandwiches, a tomato, with yoghurt and an orange for afters.

The protein in tuna fish helps our bodies to grow properly and stay in good repair. If you fall over and cut yourself your body will use protein to make new skin. Meat, fish, eggs, cheese, nuts, beans and lentils all contain protein.

Anna believes that it is wrong to eat meat. We say she is a vegetarian. Her rice salad with beans and nuts gives her body-building protein. The beans and nuts also contain fibre. We need fibre to help us keep healthy and to stop us from getting constipated.

Fibre is in many fruits and vegetables as well as in wholemeal bread and some breakfast cereals. Her banana also contains fibre.

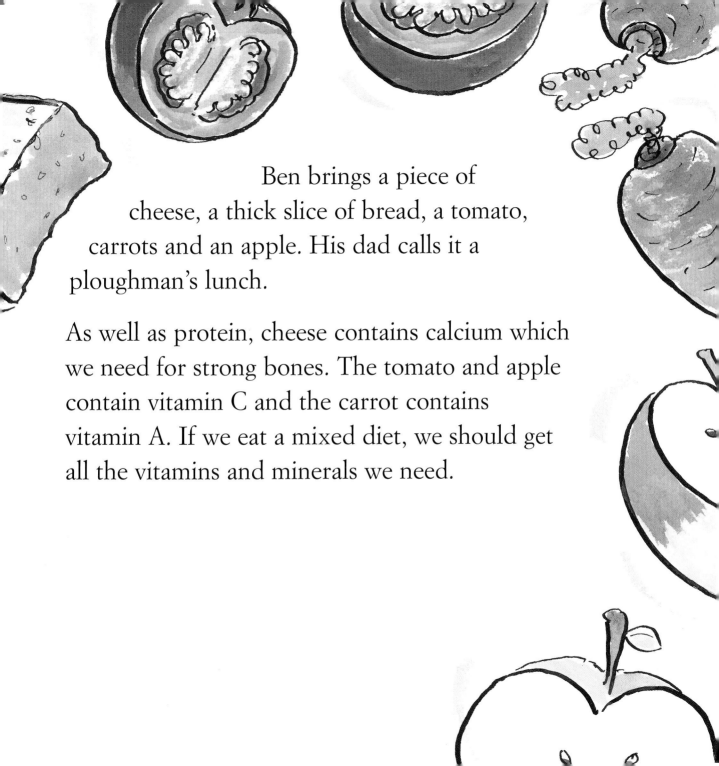

Ben brings a piece of cheese, a thick slice of bread, a tomato, carrots and an apple. His dad calls it a ploughman's lunch.

As well as protein, cheese contains calcium which we need for strong bones. The tomato and apple contain vitamin C and the carrot contains vitamin A. If we eat a mixed diet, we should get all the vitamins and minerals we need.

Justin has peanut butter sandwiches with jam – his favourite. His mum wouldn't let him bring a chocolate biscuit, because he's already had jam. She says eating sugary foods too often is bad for your teeth. Instead he has yoghurt and a tangerine.

He has to remember to take a pill at lunchtime, so he brings that in his lunch box too.

Kelly's mum has given her a grilled sausage, with rolls and lettuce.

Her mum says it is better to grill food when you can, as it's not good to eat too much fried food, and they had chips for supper last night.

To keep healthy, some people must always avoid certain foods.

Jemma has diabetes. She has to be careful about what and when she eats. Today she has chicken sandwiches with tomato and cucumber. She has also brought two satsumas and an apple. She had a digestive biscuit at breaktime.

Rashida's mum has made her meat and vegetable samosas. Rashida can't eat eggs or nuts, they make her very ill. She knows not to taste Justin's sandwiches. She even has to be careful not to touch the nuts on the bird table, in case she licks her fingers afterwards.

When she and her mum go shopping they read the labels carefully to make sure they don't buy food that might contain nuts. Even tiny amounts can make her very poorly. She has to be extra careful to ask before she eats anything at parties.

Tony has brought a thick slice of pizza, with cheese, ham and tomatoes on top. He has a packet of crisps and an orange. He's only allowed crisps once a week.

Kate has brought ham and salad sandwiches, yoghurt and a banana. She has a cereal bar in case she's still hungry.

A few months ago Kate was always tired. She didn't like getting up in the mornings, so she hardly had time for breakfast.

Mum was worried, she took Kate to the doctor. He said she was feeling tired because she missed breakfast and so she didn't get enough energy in the morning. Now she has cereal with milk – and toast and jam before she comes to school. She feels much better.

Class 3c are doing a topic on food. They have made some posters.

The Calcium in milk makes our bones and nails grow strong
Sugary foods are bad for our teeth
CHOC
Toffee
We Shouldn't eat these foods too often
Jam
Pop
FIZZ
Sunlight helps our skin to make Vitamin D
BUT BE CAREFUL NOT TO BURN IN THE SUN

THE BALANCE OF GOOD HEALTH

Fruit and Vegetables

Bread, other cereals and potatoes

Meat, fish and other proteins

Foods containing fat, foods containing sugar

Milk and dairy foods

Healthy eating means having three meals a day, starting with breakfast, and eating a variety of different foods.

If you are using a lot of energy you may need an extra snack between meals. Jason has a glass of milk. Sam's mum gives him a pear and a scone.

Further reading:

Enjoy Healthy Eating, the Balance of Good Health

Published by
The Health Education Authority

Sales and distribution:
HEA Customer Services,
Marston Book Services,
PO Box 269,
Oxon, OX14 4YN

Tel: 01235 465565
Fax: 01235 465556